THE BLACK COU

Volume 2

A Second Portrait in Old Picture Postcards

by

Eric Woolley

S.B. Publications
1990

Dedicated to the people of the Black Country

First published in 1990 by S. B. Publications

5 Queen Margaret's Road, Loggerheads, Nr. Market Drayton, Shropshire, TF9 4EP.

ISBN 1 870708 48 2

Typeset and Printed in Great Britain by Manchester Free Press, Paragon Mill, Jersey Street, Manchester, M4 6FP. Tel: 061-236 8822.

CONTENTS

CONTENTS CONTINUED

CONTENTS CONTINUED

CONTENTS CONTINUED

CONTENTS CONTINUED

ACKNOWLEDGEMENTS

The author is indebted to the many helpful people he met in the streets of the area and, also, to the following people without whom this book would not have been possible:
Alan Trevitt Smith, for the loan of several postcards;
John Madison, West Bromwich Library;
The libraries at Cradley Heath and Tipton;
Ma Pardoes, Netherton;
Short Heath Methodist Church;
The caretaker, St Giles' Church;
Gillian Jackson, for editing the text;
Steve Benz, for additional editing and marketing.

INTRODUCTION

The postcard collecting "bug" is not a new diversion into the world of nostalgia. I have been interested in postcards for more than twenty years and am still finding views of the area that I have not come across before — although the better cards of the Black Country are much scarcer these days.

To collectors, the period from 1902 to 1915 has become known as the Golden Age of the picture postcard. Millions were produced during this period and these were either used for correspondence or were avidly collected and saved. Almost every household had an album of cards for visitors to admire and the post office had least six collections a day — the last one often being as late as 7 p.m. It was not until World War 1 ended that postcard production and usage declined. This was partly due to increased postage rates and the greater availability of telephones.

Following the success of my first book on the area. I was delighted to be asked to prepare a second volume of my beloved Black Country. The sequence of postcards has been chosen to follow a similar route to that in Volume 1, with a few miscellaneous scenes at the end. I trust that this book will bring back more happy memories to those old enough to remember the "Good Old Days", and give readers as much pleasure as I have had in selecting the postcards.

Eric Woolley
June 1990

THE AUTHOR

Eric Woolley was born in Willenhall and at the local Central Boys' School. He has collected postcards since 1971 and, with the help of his wife, Wyn, has assembled a rare and extensive collection. Following his redundancy in 1982, Eric turned his hobby in to a business — E. W. Postcards, buying and selling postcards and travelling all over the country, attending numerous postcard fairs. Eric is also the author of three other local books in this series: *The Black Country,* published in 1988 and reprinted in 1989 and 1990; *Wolverhampton,* published in 1989 and reprinted in 1990 and *Walsall,* published in 1989.

COLTHAM ROAD, SHORT HEATH, c.1912

The area as Short Heath is on the very edge of the Black Country, just a couple of miles from Willenhall. This postcard shows Coltham Road, which is probably one of the better-known roads in Short Heath. Whilst an elderly woman poses for the photographer, the three small children seem unaware of this as they play in the traffic-free road. Behind the children, the side wall of the building has enamel advertisements for Coleman's starch and Lyons tea. In the right foreground is the facade of F E Brooks' grocery and post office, shown on the next page.

COLTHAM ROAD, SHORT HEATH, c.1912

Another view of the road shows the street looking from the opposite direction. Mr F E Brooks doubled up as a grocer and sub-postmaster and ran this shop for many years. He can be seen standing in the shop doorway; the post-box is set in the wall beyond, below a sign which reads "Public Telephone". The shop windows have displays of household goods and advertisements for Rinso soap and Fry's cocoa. Several people in the street seem to have noticed the photographer.

Unfortunately, no clue is given to his identity or that of the publishers of these postcards.

WESLEYAN CHURCH, SHORT HEATH, c.1912

The Wesleyan Church is rarely seen on postcards. Here the trees are bare of leaves allowing a good view of the Church and its tower. The present building is the third chapel to be used. The foundation stone was laid by Mr Tildesley on 11th July, 1881, and the building costs totalled about £2,000. The new chapel was opened officially on 5th April, 1882, and celebrated its centenary in 1981. Note the horse-drawn milk cart, complete with milk churns, standing under the street lamp on the left of the photograph.

Bus Terminus, Willenhall.

THE BUS TERMINUS, WILLENHALL, c.1937

A wealth of detail is shown on this postcard. The trolley-bus from Wolverhampton would turn around the island to make its return journey - not without mishaps though, as the poles would often leave the overhead cables and splay wildly until the bus conductor, with the use of a large pole, replaced them! On the left, the Dale cinema has a poster advertising "O'Shaughnessy's Boy", starring Wallace Beery and Jackie Cooper. The building with the curved frontage is the old Trustee Savings Bank and, on the opposite side, the Midland Bank stands on the corner of New Road and Market Place.

THE MARKET PLACE, WILLENHALL, c.1918

This fine photographic postcard is unusual as most views of the Market Place were taken from its opposite end. A street market has been held here for as long as people can remember. On the extreme left is The Bell public house with Rigby's Stores beyond. In the centre of the view is Thornley's Cash Stores with two delightful advertisements for Milkmaid milk above the shop's sign. Just visible, behind the clock, is Henly & Co.'s hardware shop with an array of buckets, laundry and gardening equipment hanging outside. These premises are still operating today.

WILLENHALL'S WORLD WAR 1 EFFORT, c.1916

Willenhall residents were very patriotic and their response to fund raising in the two World Wars was magnificent. This postcard shows crowds thronging the Market Place to listen to the military band and to hear the announcement of the final total collected for the war effort — the magnificent sum of £204,309. Note the bunting stretched to the four corners of the clock, from both sides of the street. The clock was erected in 1812, in memory of Joseph Tonks; a well known and respected doctor in the town.

THE TOWN HALL, WALSALL ROAD, WILLENHALL, c.1950

The new Town Hall was built in 1935, at a cost of almost £12,000. It replaced the original Town Hall which was converted for use as the public library. The town's fire station adjoins the Town Hall, on the right of this view. On the left of the picture, behind the Town Hall, are the municipal swimming baths, which were built in 1938 and, during the winter months, were used as an assembly hall by covering the pool with a sprung maple wood floor. The library has now been in the Town Hall building since Willenhall became part of the borough of Walsall.

NEW CHURCH SCHOOLS, WALSALL ROAD, WILLENHALL, c.1908
This school was opened in 1908 and replaced the old ones that stood on grounds which were once a garden site, at the junction of Doctors Piece and Lower Lichfield Street. The school is still in use and now incorporates a nursery. This photographic postcard was published by the local firm of Cartwright Brothers.

"Old Oak" Bowling Green, Willenhall

Headquarters "Old Oak" Inn, Walsall Road Sampson Wakelam, Proprietor

THE OLD OAK BOWLING GREEN, WALSALL ROAD, WILLENHALL, c.1909
Bowling has always been a popular sport in the Black Country. Many of the public houses in the area had their own greens at the rear of the building and the Old Oak Inn was no exception. At the time of this picture, the proprietor was a Mr Sampson Wakelam. The members were obviously very proud of their clubhouse and immaculate green.

WILLENHALL COACHCRAFT, WALSALL ROAD, WILLENHALL, c.1936
This very rare postcard shows the garage and forecourt of Willenhall Coachcraft. The business was started by Mr Joe Knight, who is pictured on the right of the old "Power" petrol pumps with an employee. Mr Knight once traded in ex-War Department vehicles of all kinds and was still the owner of the business in the mid-1970s. Now in his eighties, he lives at Penkridge. The business is still conducted from these premises by two local gentlemen, who remember that the garage was once nicknamed "Willenhall Witchcraft" by a lady who lived opposite. The business is now motor-car sales, with a franchise from Audi and Volkswagen.

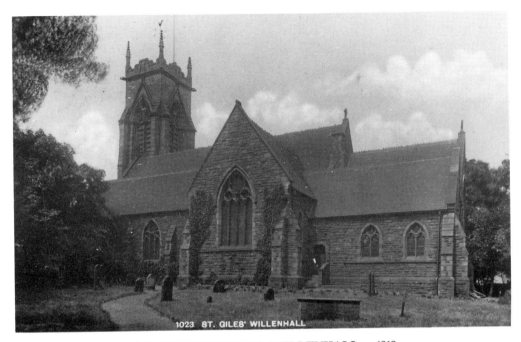

1023 ST. GILES' WILLENHALL

ST. GILES' CHURCH, WILLENHALL, c.1919

The Church is comprised within, and co-extensive with, the Ancient Chapelry of Willenhall. The Church was a former chapel of ease to its mother church in Wolverhampton. It was rebuilt in 1867 and cost almost £7,000. Built of stone in the Decorative style, it consists of a chancel, nave, aisles, transepts, west porch and a tower which is almost 100 ft. high and contains eight bells and a clock. The church stands on the site of a building which was erected most probably at the beginning of the 14th century.

THE TUMBLEDOWN BRIDGE, RAILWAY LANE, WILLENHALL, 1933

A rare view of the inn clearly shows the fine detail of its signs. The landlord was Arthur Wheatley, a well-known personality in the town, who was famous for breeding fox-terrier dogs. The inn was very popular, especially during the summer months, as it was near to the open fields known as the "Long Acres", which were on the walk from Portobello to Willenhall. Sadly, the inn is no longer there but the bridge still spans the railway line.

GREAT WESTERN RAILWAY STAFF, WILLENHALL, c.1914

This photographic postcard depicts the cartage staff of the Great Western Railway goods depot at Stafford Street Station. There are six men in the picture, but only five horses, so one of them would have been the yard foreman — probably the second man from the left, as he is dressed a little differently from the others. Three of the men are wearing long aprons under their jackets.

The station has not been used for many years and new houses have been built on the site.

THE WATERGLADE INN, BILSTON ROAD, WILLENHALL

THE WATERGLADE INN, BILSTON ROAD, WILLENHALL, c.1910

According to the printed message on the reverse of this postcard, the Waterglade was only one minute's walk from the London & North Western Railway station and the electric trams passed constantly. It had beautifully laid out gardens at the back of the house and could be used as accommodation for parties and cyclists. The proprietor was Alf Rowledge, who boasted "Fine Home Brewed Ales, Wines and Spirits and Cigars of the finest quality". There is still a public house that is known as the Waterglade, but it is unrecognisable when compared with this picture.

HIGH STREET, BILSTON, c.1908

The High Street captured on a winter's day by the cameraman of John Price & Sons of Bilston. A group of children are determined to be included in the picture! They are standing near the well-known shop of Southan Bros — note the fine gas-lamps on the front. On the extreme left there is a butcher's shop with poultry hanging outside. Further up the street is a branch of Bon Marche. The road looks extremely dirty and the tram-lines can only just be seen in the centre of the road — perhaps there had been a slight fall of snow. Today, the High Street is a busy shopping centre, with the new Market Hall and shopping precinct.

LICHFIELD STREET, BILSTON, c.1925

The cinema — or Picture Palace — was owned by T R Woods who was a councillor and also chairman of the Bilston Nursing Association. The main films showing at the time of this view were "The Only Woman" starring Norma Talmadge, the most famous of three sisters who were stars of silent films, and "Helen's Baby" starring Baby Peggy, a child star of the 1920s. The cinema opened nightly from 6 pm to 10.30 pm with matinees on Mondays and Thursdays at 2.30 pm. The Palace café was in the adjacent building. The Picture Palace subsequently became the Odeon cinema and is now a bingo hall.

Oxford St. Bilston, Staffs.

OXFORD STREET, BILSTON, c.1951

On the left of this view — which is looking towards Moxley — is the Oak & Ivy public house, selling Trumans Burton Ales. Today, this is the only one of these buildings which is still standing. On the right, there is a newsagent's shop with a large board advertising the magazine "Illustrated" and signs for popular brands of cigarettes including Wills' Capstan, Players and Park Drive. Oxford Street was once a busy shopping area but, due to progress and redevelopment, has succumbed to the full force of the demolisher. The new "Black Country Route" will cross this area near Queen Street, which is on the left-hand side with the Ship & Rainbow on the corner.

CAMBRIDGE STREET, BILSTON, c.1902

Cambridge Street ran from Green Croft to the Crescent. All these terrace houses have gone to make way for modern dwellings. This early photographic postcard shows a quiet scene, although a well-dressed lady with a pushchair and a small boy, wearing a white apron, pose for the photograph.

THE LABURNUMS, BILSTON, c.1933

This lovely old house and garden stood in Prouds Lane. It was purchased for the ex-servicemen of the town, to be used as a club known as The War Memorial Club. The grounds were open to the public and sometimes used for garden parties and other functions. After the house was demolished in the 1950s, the site was utilised for Bilston's new swimming baths and leisure complex.

LIBERAL DEMONSTRATION AT BILSTON.
JUNE 20TH, 1914.

LIBERAL DEMONSTRATION AT BILSTON, 20th June, 1914

The Liberals conducted this meeting where the main speaker was Mr Max Muspratt, the local Liberal candidate at the time. Also represented at the the meeting was a contingent of Hurst Hill Liberals, who hoisted a placard pronouncing "Hurst Hill for Progress" — the edge of the placard is just visible on the left-hand side of the picture. Hurst Hill is a parish between Bilston and Sedgeley.

BILSTON FIRE BRIGADE, c.1928

There was a smart turnout by the firefighters of Bilston when they posed for this photograph! The fire station was situated in Market Street until the redevelopment of the old market, when the Fire Brigade moved to new buildings in Prosser Street.

ALL SAINTS CHURCH, MOXLEY, c.1909

All Saints Church was built in 1850-1851 and cost £3,200 to erect. A spire and the upper part of the tower were added in 1887 by T and C Wells in memory of their father. A stone altar was built in 1926 financed by a Mrs Brookes in memory of her son, Harry. The postcard was sent in December, 1909, and the message concerns the problems of moving house. It states: "...I don't want to go into any more rooms" — which is underlined — "...Surely you can get ready for Jan 3rd...have the front room as fine as you can & don't bother about the back. Yes, lino will do..."

MOXLEY WESLEYANS FOOTBALL CLUB, 1923-4

Many local churches and chapels formed football teams and this rare postcard shows the lads who represented the Wesleyan Chapel, Moxley, during the season 1923-4. They won two trophies — which are displayed here — and several of their team progressed to the higher standard of the Football League. The photograph was taken at the rear of a house and, on the right, there are a couple of people peering over the wall, watching the cameraman — and hoping to be included in the picture!

DARLASTON, c.1939

Five views of the town for the price of one picture postcard! In the centre of this multiview is St. Lawrence's Church and, surrounding it are views of Victoria Park, King Street, Victoria Road and the entrance to George Ross Park. Each of these pictures could also be bought as a single view postcard; they were published by Masons of the Bull Stake.

THE BULL STAKE, DARLASTON, c.1907

The Bull Stake takes its name from the former practise of bull-baiting which took place here. Situated at the junction of Walsall Road, Wednesbury Road, Pinfold Street and King Street, it was a busy shopping area of the town. On the right, the shops have goods displayed on the pavements and there are many potential customers walking down the street. The cart on the left is from Dudley and is waiting by a tram-stop. Here, the tram-lines divide to form a passing loop up the hill in King Street. In the foreground, there is a fine old post-box beneath the lamp standard. The town coat of arms is shown on the bottom right-hand corner of the card.

25

BULL PIECE, DARLASTON

No 36

THE BULL PIECE, DARLASTON, c.1915

The Bull Piece shown looking towards Victoria Road. The spire of St. Lawrence's Church can be seen in the background. Note the early bollards and street lamp which form a small island at the junction. A horse-drawn vehicle approaches from the bridge which crosses the railway cutting.

VICTORIA ROAD, DARLASTON

VALENTINES SERIES

79198

VICTORIA ROAD, DARLASTON, c.1912

Victoria Road is seen here from the opposite direction to that shown on the multiview (see page 24). In the centre of this picture is the Swan Hotel which is well over one hundred years old. Nearer the camera there is a tobacconist with many advertisements for well-known brands: St. Bruno, St. Julien, Guinea Gold, Wills and Coolie Cut Plug. The little shop on the right is a family butcher, but appears to be closed. Although the street is quiet, a man is riding a heavy horse up the main road, and there are several pedestrians around. The Town Hall and Post Office are among notable buildings in this road.

THE WAR MEMORIAL, DARLASTON, c.1927

The memorial was erected to remember the local men who gave their lives during the Great War of 1914-18. It stands in the grounds of the Park, at the junction of Victoria Road and Slater Street. As the photograph was taken in the summertime and, as there are numerous poppy wreaths laid around the cenotaph, it is probable that this photograph was taken shortly after the unveiling ceremony. The names of those men killed in World War 2 have since been added to the memorial.

WAR MEMORIAL, DARLASTON.   No 5.

GORDON STREET, DARLASTON, c.1935

This postcard was published by B.D. Smith a newsagent and stationer of Walsall Road, Wednesbury. It appears to have been a very quiet street with the only noticeable animation being a horse-drawn vehicle in the distance, and the small boy who seems to be pushing an early type of pushchair.

CLASS 1, DORSET ROAD SCHOOL, DARLASTON, 7th October, 1920

This card brings back memories of old school days! It shows the pupils and their teacher who seem to have been photographed during an art lesson as each child has a blank sheet of paper and paintbox, with a clean pot of water on each desk. The two children from the front desk are standing at the back with their teacher. These old wood and iron desks, with holes for inkwells, accommodated two pupils. This is a large class of over fifty pupils — three are squashed into one of the front desks. Note how children used to sit up straight with their hands behind them and note the expressions on some of their faces! This school is now the Joseph Cox primary school.

Plate Girder leaving JESSE TILDESLEY LTD.
Crescent Iron Works,
:: *DARLASTON.* ::

WEIGHT. 72 TONS.   112 FEET LONG.

CRESCENT IRON WORKS, DARLASTON, c.1935

The caption on this postcard states that the photograph is of a plate girder leaving the Crescent Iron Works of Jesse Tildesley Ltd., manufacturers of steel bridges. The works was situated on Willenhall Road. The girder in the picture weighed 72 tons and was 112 feet long. Many of the ironworkers can be seen sitting on the top of the girder, posing for the cameraman.

J & R ROSE LTD.,
LONDON WORKS, DARLASTON
12th March, 1936

James and Richard Rose were manufacturers of railway and carriage coach bolts. Most of this unusual postcard depicts the tray that was presented to the Managing Director of J & R Rose Ltd., by the works' employees. The inset photograph shows the ceremony. The tray is engraved to:

"Frederick William Butler Esq.
Chairman & Managing Director
as a mark of esteem & respect
12th March 1936".

IMPERIAL WORKS FOOTBALL CLUB, DARLASTON, 1922-3

These men were members of the football team from the Imperial Works. No trophies are on display, so the picture was probably taken at the start of the season. The Imperial Works were owned by Charles Richards Ltd., nut and bolt manufacturers.

MUNICIPAL BUILDINGS, HOLYHEAD ROAD, WEDNESBURY, c.1915
The Town Hall was erected in 1871-2, enlarged in 1913, and also used for social functions. The
General Post Office is adjacent to the Town Hall — on the left of this view. There are two posting
slots beneath the window, one for newspapers and the other for letters.

Market Place, Wednesbury.

MARKET PLACE, WEDNESBURY, c.1917

This view shows the Market Place looking towards the square. A tram can be seen as it passes the clock which was erected to commemorate the Coronation of King George V. The picture gives a good view of the various shops in the town, at that time. On the left are: Boots the Chemists, the Central Café, the Maypole and the drapery belonging to F W Preece. On the right-hand side is Longmore's, a high-class gentlemen's outfitter, with a sign for Jaeger wear in the doorway.

Wednesbury Market.

Ryder & Son.

WEDNESBURY MARKET, c.1903

On market days, the Market Place was teeming with people and activity. This view shows the area from the opposite direction to that on the previous page. A very busy scene, with crowds of shoppers vying for any would-be bargains from the many and varied covered stalls.

MARKET PLACE, WEDNESBURY, c.1939

On the left-hand side of this real photographic view is Collins' boot and shoe shop, with rows of shoes suspended from a rail over the window. Next door is a newsagent's shop that was possibly also a post office, as a pillar-box stands on the pavement outside it. On the opposite side of the street, there are some larger shops including a branch of F W Woolworth. Outside the adjacent bank, a horse waits patiently between the shafts of his cart. On the right, the motor-car seems to have the parking area to itself.

CO-OPERATIVE SOCIETY GALA, MARKET PLACE, WEDNESBURY, c.1914
The Market Place again — but this time there is an entirely different scene as people crowd the area for the local children's gala. A banner draped on the clock tower gives this information, together with the total sum raised at the previous year's gala — £15,000. There are some horse-drawn floats at the rear of the crowd and a cartload of children in front of Foster's Clothing Store. The placards that are being held up identify the branches of the Co-op. This postcard was published by the local photographer J W Bernard of 26 Union Street, Wednesbury.

PUBLIC LIBRARY, WEDNESBURY, c.1940

The site for a library was presented by the former Mayor and Mayoress, Alderman Handley and his wife. The building was erected in 1907-8 and cost £7,000. The Andrew Carnegie Trust donated the sum of £5,636 towards the building costs. The picture shows Walsall Road with the Library on the corner of Hollies Drive, where the main entrance is situated. As the photograph was taken in wartime, the Library has been protected by sandbags which have been stacked up to the level of the first-floor windows.

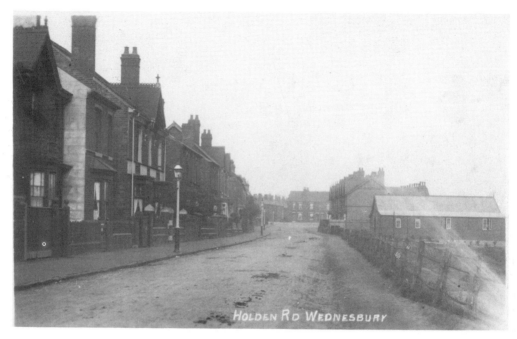

HOLDEN ROAD, WEDNESBURY, c.1913

According to Hackwood, the well-known Wednesbury historian, Holden Road was once known as "Hangmans Lane" because the manorial execution elm stood here. This rare view shows Holden Road looking towards Hydes Road. On the right is the old golf course and clubhouse, the site of which has since been used for residential development.

THE CONSERVATIVE CLUB, WEDNESBURY, c.1905

The local Conservative Club was established in 1886 and their club premises were rebuilt in 1904 in Walsall Street, opposite the top of Spring Head. It is stated that the club had every convenience for an institution of its kind. The postcard was published by the Wednesbury firm or Ryder & Son of the Herald Office. A photograph has been superimposed with an artist's impression of a horse-drawn cab passing the building; except for the man on the left, the pedestrians have also been drawn onto the photograph.

GREAT WESTERN HOTEL, WEDNESBURY, c.1923

Situated on the corner of Potter Street and Great Western Street, this Hotel bears the old trademark of Mitchells and Butlers brewery. The "Deer's Leap", as it is known throughout the Black Country, can be seen very clearly, here. The partners in the brewery, Henry Mitchell and William Butler, started the firm in 1898. The Hotel has now gone.

THE PARK, WEDNESBURY, c.1914

The site for Brunswick Park was purchased from the Patent Shaft and Axletree Company at a cost of £3,000, and is 28 acres in size. It was opened on 21st June, 1887, to celebrate Queen Victoria's Golden Jubilee and, much to the delight of the local inhabitants, was dedicated to the people of Wednesbury. The Wednesbury coat of arms is portrayed in the bottom right-hand corner of the postcard.

The cross indicates a cottage off Bridge Street, once the home of "Honest Munchin," a converted ruffian who rescued John Wesley from his would-be murderers in the historic Wednesbury riots in 1743. He died at Birmingham in 1789, at the age of 85, and his tombstone may be seen in St. Paul's Churchyard there.

Honest Munchin's Cottage, Wednesbury.   Ryder &

HONEST MUNCHIN'S COTTAGE, WEDNESBURY,
c.1907

George Munchin is famous locally for his efforts during the Wednesbury riots, in 1743, when he helped the non-conformist Wesleyen minister, John Wesley, to escape a mob who were intent on taking his life. After this act, Munchin became a friend of the minister. George's real name was George Clifton, but his nickname of Honest Munchin lives on. His cottage was just off Bridge Street and is marked with a cross on this view. Munchin died in 1789 and his tombstone can be seen in St. Paul's Churchyard, in Birmingham. This postcard, with a brief life history, was also published by the local firm, Ryder & Son.

THE CANAL FROM CRANKHALL BRIDGE, WEDNESBURY, c.1906

Another printed postcard from the firm of Ryder & Son shows the Tame Valley Canal from Crankhall
Bridge. The solitary horse-drawn barge seems as if it was superimposed onto the picture, as not
a ripple can be seen in the water.

COSELEY CANAL TUNNEL

CANAL TUNNEL, COSELEY,
c.1908

A lovely postcard from John Price & Sons "stable" shows a horse-drawn canal barge leaving the tunnel at the Ivy House Lane end. The original line of the canal wound round Coseley Hill. The tunnel was constructed when Thomas Telford was appointed to shorten James Brindley's original canal. By incorporating several cuttings and tunnels, the route between Birmingham and Wolverhampton was shortened by some seven miles. This tunnel is 360 yards long and has a towpath on each side. It runs from Ivy House Lane to School Street. A public house, known locally as the Puzzle Gardens, was near the School Street end. According to a local legend, if children suffering from whooping-couth walked the length of this tunnel, they were magically cured of the disease!

PROVIDENCE
BAPTIST CHAPEL,
COSELEY.

—

BUILT 1871.

—

CHURCH FORMED
ABOUT 1805.

PROVIDENCE BAPTIST CHAPEL, COSELEY, c.1913

This is a very rare postcard. The Baptist Chapel was built in 1871, but the church had been formed many years earlier, around 1805. In recent years the Chapel has had extensive alterations and refurbishments.

"The Beacon Hill was crowned with a garland of Nature's own weaving, and under the noble shelter of its luxuriant foliage the Druid priests had oft performed their mystic rites." Lawley's *History of Bilston.*

BEACON HILL AND MONUMENT, SEDGLEY, c.1921

A man ploughs the acres with a horse-drawn plough on this lovely rural scene. In the distance is the monument on Beacon Hill, which is 654 feet above sea level. A typical piece of text on the postcard sums up the picture: "The Beacon Hill was crowned with a garland of Nature's own weaving, and under the noble shelter of its luxuriant foliage the Druid priests had oft performed their mystic rites". Lawley's *History of Bilston.*

MEMORIAL CALVARY, SEDGLEY, c.1920

This unusual cenotaph stands in the churchyard of St. Mary the Virgin. It was erected in memory of the men of Hurst Hill who gave their lives for King and Country in the Great War of 1914-18. The small text on the bottom of the plinth reads "Rest eternal grant unto them O Lord and let light perpetual shine upon them".

St Mary The Virgin, Sedgley. (Memorial Calvary)

Roman Catholic Church, Sedgley.

ROMAN CATHOLIC CHURCH, DUDLEY ROAD, SEDGLEY, c.1908
The first Roman Catholic Church at Sedgley was built in 1789. The one in the picture was erected in 1823, and was consecrated to Saint Chad and All Saints in 1891. It has a high altar and reredos carved from stone.

ELLOWES HALL, SEDGLEY.   540.

ELLOWES HALL, SEDGLEY, c.1915

The "Ellowes" was built in 1821 on an estate owned by the Fereday family. John Turton Fereday bought the estate from his uncle, Samuel Fereday, a well-known ironmaster. In 1846, financial problems forced John to sell the house to his son-in-law, John Latty Bickley, who never settled in it. William Baldwin from Bilston was the next owner, in the early 1850s. There were several more occupants until, in 1931, the condition of the house had deteriorated so much, that the owners could not afford its upkeep and turned it into flats. After use by the Home Guard during World War 2, the estate was sold. The vandalised, listed building had to be demolished in 1964.

Cottage at Baggeridge Woods.

BAGGERIDGE WOODS, c.1907

A snow-bound cottage in the local beauty spot was a good subject for this postcard which was used to convey Christmas greetings. The area was very popular with the people of the Black Country and, nowadays, it has its own nature trail. Baggeridge was the site of the last of the Earl of Dudley's collieries. It is also world-famous for the "Baggeridge building brick".

INTERIOR, WESLEYAN CHAPEL, GORNAL WOOD.

Davies' Post Card Series, No.

THE WESLEYAN CHAPEL, GORNAL WOOD, c.1906

In the Black Country, the Wesleyan movement was very strong and churches and chapels sprang up all around the area. The Chapel is a very attractive building with flower beds around the entrance. It was erected in 1827 and rebuilt in 1895. This picture is a typical example of a chapel interior. The message on the reverse of the postcard states: "One more Methodist card for your collection", which indicates that postcards of all sorts and themes were collected during the Edwardian era.

LOWER GORNAL SILVER BAND, c.1938

The Lower Gornal Primitive Methodist Silver Band pose for the camera. They are dressed in their magnificent uniforms — all except for the young boy seated at the front and the two gentlemen on either side of the bandmaster. The insignia of the band is painted on the big drum.

THE CAVERN, WREN'S NEST,
c.1915

The postcard was published by Tipton's best-known photographer, William Haddon, who has managed to capture a very elegant-looking lady standing by the mouth of the cavern in an otherwise barren scene. As mentioned in Volume 1, the area is a maze of caverns and holes; these were created by quarrying and mining for sandstone, lime and other rich deposits. The area is known as a classic exposure of Upper Silurian limestone and over 300 species of fossil fauna are represented here. The fossils were first noted in 1686, and are known to be over 300 million years old. The site is the only geological nature reserve in England.

CAVERN, WRENS NEST, DUDLEY. HADDON SERIES

55

ENTRANCE TO VICTORIA PARK, TIPTON.

OWEN STREET, TIPTON.

TIPTON, c.1911

The top view shows the entrance to Victoria Park. The land for a park was purchased in 1897, to commemorate Queen Victoria's Diamond Jubilee. It cost £1,500 and this sum was raised by public subscription. The Park was opened in 1902, by the Earl of Dartmouth. The bottom picture shows Owen Street, with the Albion Inn on the left and a hay, straw and corn warehouse on the right. This street has changed considerably; most of the shops have gone and have been replaced by new dwellings and flats for a canal-side development.

OWEN STREET, TIPTON, c.1946

Looking down the street, this very interesting scene is rich in content. The Fountain public house still attracts attention on the junction with Factory Road. It is one of the Black Country's oldest buildings and many people believe that it should be protected by being graded as a listed building. The sign bears the picture of William Perry, better known as the "Tipton Slasher", the Black Country's famous prize-fighter. When this photograph was taken, there was no problem parking in the town centre — if one was wealthy enough to own a car!

SEDGLEY ROAD, TIPTON, c.1905

The road is almost deserted in this view that was printed by the firm of Elton and Brown of Tipton. Today, this is built-up area, with houses on the land on the right, and the road is a busy traffic route. The postcard was sent from Tipton to Cork in Ireland, on the eve of St. Patrick's Day, 1905, and the message reads: "Many thanks for the splendid box of Shamrock......".

TIPTON FREE LIBRARY.

TIPTON FREE LIBRARY, c.1906
The Free Library stands in Victoria Road. It was a gift from the well-known benefactor, Andrew
Carnegie. The magnificent building was officially opened to the public in 1906.

Tipton's War Memorial, Unveiled by Marquis of Cambridge.

UNVEILING OF THE WAR MEMORIAL, TIPTON, 24th August, 1921

Standing in the park at Tipton, the cenotaph was erected to honour the dead of the Great War of 1914-18. On 24th August, 1921, it was unveiled by the Marquis of Cambridge, who was patron of the Midland Counties Area of the Royal British Legion. Among those attending the ceremony were: Admiral Cumming; Col. Commmandant Benson; Lord Dartmouth; local Member of Parliament, Alfred Short; and the Chairman of the council, W W Doughty, who was also the presiding officer. A large crowd watched the proceedings as the dedication by Reverends Mortimore, Kewley and Burford took place. The names of those killed in World War 2 have since been added to the memorial.

THE NURSES' HOME, TIPTON, c.1909

The postcard was published as a souvenir item for the visit of the King's neice, Princess Aribert, who performed the opening ceremony at the Nurses' Home on 3rd August, 1909. The Princess was Louise, the daughter of the Duke of Schleswig-Holstein and Princess Helena, Queen Victoria's fifth child. Louise was married to Prince Aribert of Anhalt. A group of the nursing staff pose in front of the home, which stood in Lower Church Lane. The postcard was published by the Birmingham firm of Russell's.

NEW ROAD, GREAT BRIDGE, c.1949

When compared with the earlier view shown in Volume 1, it is apparent that the buildings have changed little, except for detail. The first two shops on the right still have the same occupants, although the facades have been altered. The Union Supply Co. were provision Specialists and have a fine new delivery van parked outside the shop. Of course, all the horse-drawn transport of the earlier view has been superseded by motorised vehicles — perhaps necessitating the pedestrian crossing! The shop on the bend is an ice-cream parlour and has the famous Persil advertisement on its end wall. This is a very busy road today.

Market Place, Great Bridge.

MARKET PLACE, GREAT BRIDGE, c.1912

Published by John Price & Sons of Bilston, and showing the Market Place taken from the pavement by the pillar-box, seen on the previous page. The many varied stalls can clearly be seen. The two shops in the background are Gilson's Boot & Shoe stores, a retail shop boasting of fifty years standing and of a good reputation, and, next door, the Central Pharmacy, owned by someone named Griffith but which was previously run by Waterston. The old gas-lamp and pillar-box, on the right, enhance the atmosphere of this scene. The market is now held on land adjacent to Market Street.

Great end Post Office, *Great Bridge.*

THE POST OFFICE, GREAT BRIDGE, c.1910

There are many people standing outside the premises of Purser the printer, which was on the corner of Brickhouse Lane. The shop at ground level also served as the Post Office, and has many advertisements and posters on its walls. The cameraman had obviously attracted the attention of the children and customers, all of whom are happy to pose outside. The open-topped tram in the centre has the words "Nectar Tea" on the front.

HORSELEY. HEATH, TIPTON.

HORSELEY HEATH, c.1919

Horseley Heath, in the parish of Tipton, is situated between Great Bridge and Dudley Port. In 1921, it had a population of only 4,363 people. It is obvious that the cameraman found a high vantage point to photograph the scene shown here, which is looking towards Dudley Port. Most of these buildings have now gone. An old drinking fountain, incorporating a street lamp, is in the right foreground. This rare postcard was published by F C Roberts of Horseley Press.

AQUEDUCT DUDLEY PORT STATION.

Woodall
Tipton.

DUDLEY PORT, c.1909

On the left of this picture are the railway bridge with the railway station and the aqueduct which carries the Birmingham Canal across the main A461 road. The Ryland Aqueduct was completely rebuilt in 1968, becuase the old aqueduct was too narrow and was hindering road improvements. The tram-lines here are hardly noticeable, but the poles supporting the overhead cables are prominent. The postcard was published by Woodall of Tipton.

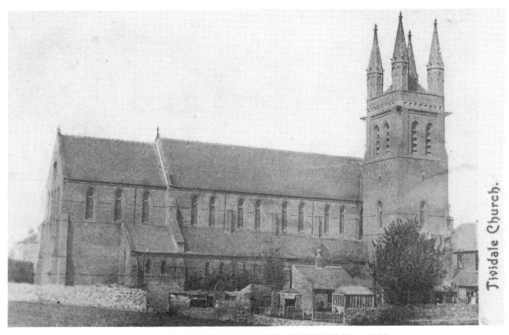

Tividale Church.

ST. MICHAEL'S CHURCH, TIVIDALE, c.1907

St. Michael's Church was built in 1887-8 and cost £11,390. It is built of brick, in the Early English style, and consists of a chancel, nave, aisles, north and south porches and a western tower with pinnacles, containing one bell. The register dates from 1874.

OLD TOWN HALL, DUDLEY.
(REMOVED 1860).

THE OLD TOWN HALL, DUDLEY

The picture is an artist's impression of the old Town Hall in the Market Place. The postcard was issued by the publisher, E Blocksidge but, unfortunately, the artist is not mentioned. The building was demolished and removed in 1860. The new Town Hall was opened in 1928 and stands at the junction of St. James Road and Priory Street.

HIGH STREET, DUDLEY, c.1910

This view is taken looking towards the market place, with the fountain in the centre of the picture. It seems that the photographer chose early-closing day, as the shop belonging to T Williams has its blinds around the windows, and there is no traffic and only a few pedestrians. A window cleaner's ladder is propped up against the wall of another building and a young boy stands between the tram-lines to be sure of being included in the photograph!

HIGH STREET, DUDLEY, c.1920

Taken from a vantage point near the top church, the picture shows, on the extreme left, a newsagent's shop which was probably also a barber's establishment, as there is a long striped pole outside. Further along, on the left-hand side, the imposing building is the headquarters of the Y.M.C.A. Just visible in the distance, a tram-car is making its way towards the cameraman. The castle can just be seen on the horizon.

POST OFFICE AND WOLVERHAMPTON STREET, DUDLEY

WOLVERHAMPTON STREET, DUDLEY, c.1929

The Post Office — on the right — is the principal building on this postcard. It is one of many fine buildings in this part of town, which is now a very busy busy throughfare. A lone motor-cyclist is the only item of traffic worthy of note.

Dudley Castle Fêtes

DUDLEY CASTLE FÊTE, c.1908
Fêtes were held in the castle grounds at Dudley and, as can be seen, these usually attracted large crowds. This is one of a series of postcards and depicts the inflation of a hot-air balloon. The gateway to the ruined castle can be seen in the background. The castle is said to have been founded in the eighth century, with the keep dating from the thirteenth century. The castle suffered a fire in 1750, but there are remains, including the barbican, two drum towers and the keep. Dudley Zoo is situated within the castle grounds.

ADVERTISING POSTCARD,
c.1910

This delightful advertising card was issued for the Dudley Laundry Co., of Queen's Cross. It bears the slogan "We return everything but the dirt". In Edwardian times, many firms used postcards to advertise their goods and services. This card was published by the Laundry Company's own advertising department and was probably one of a series.

THE DUDLEY LAUNDRY CO.,
QUEENS X, DUDLEY.

"We return everything but the dirt."

73

Canal Tunnel, Dudley.

THE CANAL TUNNEL, DUDLEY, c.1908

The picture shows a fully-loaded canal boat emerging out of the Dudley tunnel. Its cargo was probably limestone, dug from the quarries around Castle Ridge. The tunnel is narrow and 3,154 yards long. It was opened in 1792, and connected the Dudley Canal to the Birmingham Canal. In the tunnel, there is a network of over 5,000 yards of underground waterway, which gave access to the quarries and mines. These underground quarries were a nineteenth-century wonder of the Black Country. When passing through the very low, narrow tunnels to the underground basin, the boatmen had to propel their craft with their legs — a practise known as "legging it".

HIGH STREET, NETHERTON, c.1916

Several children seem to have noticed the photographer who took this picture — as have some of the shopkeepers and tradespeople, on the right. The right-hand shop is a grocery and has the awning extented to protect the goods on display in the window which has signs for Rowntree's, butter and tea. The next shop has a barber's pole outside but no visible name on the shop. On the left is the Castle Hotel or Inn belonging to Thomas Hodgkiss, a coal miner from Bilston. An old brewery stood at the rear of the building. A new public house, The Mash Tun, was built on the site by Ansells Brewery during the 1950s. The postcard was sent by Fred and Kate, who lived at 2, Campden House, Cinder Bank.

HALESOWEN ROAD, NETHERTON, c.1910

In this fascinating view, a single-deck tram approaches, in the centre, on its way from Dudley. The covered wagon on the right-hand side belonged to Barlow & Sons. The first shop is a newsagent's, with placards outside the shop and the house next door. The shop beyond belongs to a cabinetmaker and upholsterer. The children on the left have stopped their game to watch the photographer.

Public Hall, Netherton, Dudley.

PUBLIC HALL, NETHERTON, c.1907
John Price & Sons of Bilston published this postcard of the imposing Public Hall. The police station was also in the vicinity, as the person who sent the card writes "My school is near to the cross I have put on the card, but I have to behave as the police station is nearby"!

HINGLEY'S WORKS, NETHERTON, c.1907

The canal shown here is the Dudley Canal, with the adjacent works of Noah Hingley and Sons Ltd. who were the makers of some of the largest anchors and chains for the world's ocean-going liners (See Volume 1). In this view, quite a few fully-loaded barges can be seen, some of which are very low in the water.

Clock Tower, West Bromwich.

THE CLOCK TOWER, CARTER'S GREEN, WEST BROMWICH, c.1909

The Farley clock tower is 65 feet high and was erected by the townspeople in memory of Alderman Farley, J.P. The sides of the tower are decorated with a medallion bust of the late Alderman, and two other panels represent the Oak House and the Municipal buildings. Behind the tower is the Wesleyan Chapel, built in 1875-6. It closed for worship in 1949 and was used as a warehouse until it was demolished in 1970. A gazetteer of 1895 describes the town thus: "....it yet is of modern growth, having risen within the last hundred years from a mere village on a barren heath". In 1801, the population was 5,687; in 1891, it was 59,474 and, in 1961, it was 95,909.

St. Matthew's, West Bromwich.

CHRISTCHURCH
WEST BROMWICH, c.1911

The postcard depicts Christchurch, but is incorrectly captioned as St. Matthew's. The publishers were a firm named Farmer's who hailed from nearby Darlaston. Christchurch is situated in High Street and was erected over a period of several years between 1821-28. It cost £200 to purchase the site and a further £18,446 for the building work. In 1878, the interior was fully restored at a cost of £4,000. Six years later, a further £600 was spent on interior decoration and repairs to the roof. The tower is 114 feet high and contains twelve bells.

BULL STREET, WEST BROMWICH, c.1913

This photographic postcard was published by Cashmores, whose shop can be identified on the extreme left of the picture. Next door is Alf Young's tailors shop, where overalls, cords and mole trousers could be purchased. Note the jackets hanging over the doorway. The next two shops are a pie house and a grocery. The little shop on the right has signs for a "Clearance Sale of Surplus Stock". Shops beyond include: Goodwins; H N Ellison, a seed merchant; Hamptons and Haslehurst, a watch-maker. This street is now an integral part of the ring road.

DARTMOUTH SQUARE, WEST BROMWICH, c.1913

Another postcard in the Cashmore Series shows Dartmouth Square with Paradise Street on the left. The tram-lines lead to the busy High Street, in the distance. Dartmouth Square was the tram terminus for the Spon Lane route, until 17th November, 1929, when the last tram made its final journey. The building in the centre, on the junction, is a restaurant serving teas and luncheons, including their "Noted Pork Pies" — which are depicted on a large sign.

BEECHES ROAD, WEST BROMWICH, c.1913

Yet another Cashmore postcard shows one the roads that was often seen on postcards. The large terraced houses on the right have balconies and are three storeys high. Opposite, the buildings appear to be individually designed. There is some activity higher up the road — it looks as if improvements to the road surface are taking place.

Beeches Road School, West Bromwich.

BEECHES ROAD SCHOOL, WEST BROMWICH, c.1904

According to the message on the reverse of this postcard, this was a day school attended by the sender, whose name was Lizzie. As can be seen, the school possessed a fine bell tower and clock. The school is still in use today.

CHURCH VALE, WEST BROMWICH, c.1920

The semi-detatched houses on the left seem to have been fairly new when this picture was taken. The half-timbered effect on the front of the houses was a popular feature at that time. A cyclist is pedalling uphill towards the cameraman. Behind him, there appears to be a horse-drawn milk cart.

BAND STAND · DARTMOUTH PARK,
WEST BROMWICH.
CASHMORE SERIES

DARTMOUTH PARK, WEST BROMWICH, c.1920
The bandstand is the central feature of this postcard photograph, taken in the Municipal park.
The 65½-acre site was presented by the Earl of Dartmouth, in 1887, on a 99-year lease, at a nominal
rent. The improvement commissioners spent £6,000 on constructing the lake, building a lodge and
laying out the grounds. The area shown here appears to have been recently planted.

HILL TOP PARK, WEST BROMWICH, c.1930

Once again, the bandstand is the main feature of the picture. These pleasure grounds were laid out by the Corporation, covering five acres of land.

MOAT ROAD, LANGLEY, c.1937

On the right is the Victoria Stores off-licence, with a clear advertisement for Alsopps Burton Ales above the entrance. On the opposite side is the local branch of Barclays Bank Ltd. and, in front of the bank, in the centre of the junction, there is an unusual crossroads road sign.

CHURCH STREET. LOOKING NORTH. BRIERLEY HILL,

CHURCH STREET LOOKING NORTH, BRIERLEY HILL, c.1929

Several professional businesses were situated in this street, including architects, accountants and, also, the offices of the local Registrar of Births, Marriages and Deaths. Other businesses included: a wireless accessories firm; dressmakers; cobblers; a beer retailer and the Old Whimsey Inn, which is no longer there. This fine photographic postcard was published by the firm of Lilywhite Ltd., for B Dudley of High Street, Brierley Hill.

297—2   THE PARISH CHURCH, BRIERLEY HILL

ST. MICHAEL'S CHURCH, BRIERLEY HILL, c.1928

St. Michael's Church was originally built in 1765, but was enlarged in 1823 and again in 1837. During the period of 1873-88, the interior was renovated, with the chancel being raised and a new pulpit installed. Among the stained glass windows that were inserted, two were given by Mr J Corbett, M.P., and several others were given by members of the congregation.

BRETTELL LANE, c.1909

Until 1966, the Lane formed the boundary between Brierley Hill and Amblecote. A tram can be seen as it trundles on its way towards Dudley. There is a horse and trap on the left-hand side of the road. Terraced houses line both sides of the road in this typical Edwardian scene.

CHRISTCHURCH, QUARRY BANK, c.1930

The ecclesiastical parish was formed on 18th September, 1844, from Kingswinford. Christchurch was erected in 1847, at a cost of £3,000. In 1897, a chancel was added at a cost of £750. The church has a small, western turret and one bell. The register dates back to 1847.

BIRMINGHAM ROAD, ROWLEY REGIS, c.1925

The postcard, published by the firm of Parkes Bros. of Blackheath, shows Birmingham Road looking towards Rowley Hill — the Parish Church can be seen on the horizon. The Methodist Church is on the left of the picture. Several small shops can be seen amongst the row of terraced houses which line either side of the road.

ST. GILES' CHURCH AFTER THE FIRE, ROWLEY REGIS, June 1913

St. Giles' was founded as early as 1199. It was rebuilt during 1840 but, at the beginning of the twentieth century, it was found to be unsafe and was condemned. A third church was built in 1904, but was burnt down on 18th June, 1913, when it was set alight during the local suffragette riots. This postcard clearly shows the damage caused by the serious fire which completely gutted the church. In 1923, a new church was erected on Rowley Hill and was dedicated to St. Michael and All Angels.

"GREETINGS FROM BLACKHEATH", c.1927

An unusual greetings postcard depicts three views of the area. At the top are the rose gardens in Haden Hill Park, with a mother and her two young children — one in a pushchair. The centre view shows the War Memorial in Powke Lane, and the bottom picture shows part of High Street.

POWKE LANE, BLACKHEATH, c.1927

Powke Lane is almost deserted in this picture — only three people walking up the left-hand pavement and a horse and cart at the bottom. The fine War Memorial can be seen standing in the cemetery, in the distance. The sender of this postcard marked a cross on the bottom right-hand corner, denoting that her school was nearby. This is now an industrial area.

HIGH STREET, OLD HILL, c.1910

This superb view was photographed and published by the local firm of Perry. On the extreme left is Paragon buildings with a gated entrance to the yard at the rear. The first shop is F W Crumpton's store, with a window advertisement for lemonade and a notice advising housewives to use Watson's soap for spring cleaning. Further up the street, a long striped pole denotes a barber's shop. Siviter's wine stores can seen at the end of the street. Also of interest is the fully-loaded, two-wheeled, horse-drawn cart on the right of the picture. This view is almost unrecognisable today, as most of these buildings have gone.

OLD HILL LIBERAL CLUB, c.1911
The Liberal Club stood in Reddal Hill Road. Later, it was also used by members from Cradley Heath. Several people — possibly the staff — have come outside for the benefit of the photographer, who was also from the local firm of Perry's.

THE FREE LIBRARY, CRADLEY HEATH, c.1909
The Library was a gift from the generous Andrew Carnegie. It cost £2,700 and opened in 1908.
It also serves the parish of Old Hill and stands in Reddal Hill Road. This postcard was issued
by the little-known firm of B R Hill of Cradley Heath.

HIGH STREET, CRADLEY HEATH, c.1909

On the right-hand side of this superb street scene, there are fashionable ladies with their children, and young boys in Eton collars and Norfolk jackets. Above them, rails of clothes are on display at Bradley's shop. Further down is Griffiths' jeweller's shop, which is still there today. In the distance, there are many people and a tram is approaching from Dudley. There are several horse-drawn vehicles and, as a result, the road is rather dirty! The street has changed over the years and many of these shops have gone.

FIVE WAYS, CRADLEY HEATH
CRADLEY HEATH

FIVE WAYS, CRADLEY HEATH, c.1907

This real photographic postcard by the local firm of E Beech is an excellent example of their work. Five Ways is the junction of five roads: Lowere High Street, High Street, Cradley Road, Graingers Lane and St. Annes Road. In the centre of the view, a lady is alighting from the tram-car, which has stopped outside the Crown Inn. There are many children dressed in Edwardian fashions. It seems that everyone in the vicintiy was prepared to stand and be included in the photograph.

PARISH CHURCH, CRADLEY HEATH.   No 9

ST. LUKE'S CHURCH, CRADLEY HEATH, c.1921

St. Luke's was built under the New Parishes Act, 1843, and was consecrated in February, 1847. It is constructed of red sandstone, in the Early English style, and consists of a chancel, nave, transepts, south porch and a western turret containing one bell. The Church was restored in 1874-5, when the apse was added and the interior rearranged, at a cost of £3,486.

F. HINGLEY'S SHOP, CRADLEY HEATH, c.1911

Uncaptioned postcards of shop fronts are difficult to identify. This rare postcard shows the shop belonging to a Mr F Hingley who was, apparently, a glass and china dealer. Could that be Mrs Hingley standing in the entrance of the shop? Note the wickerwork baskets hanging in the doorway. The window display shows some fine examples of what are today's antiques.

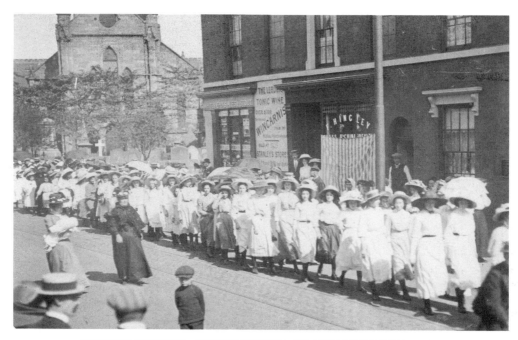

SUNDAY SCHOOL ANNIVERSARY, CRADLEY HEATH, c.1911

Hingley's shop appears on this postcard as well! The young girls all wore white dresses for this occasion, and turn to look at the photographer as they pass by. The corner shop is a wine store, the proprietor being a Mr Stanley; the advertisement on the wall is for Wincarnis tonic wine, at 3/6d. a bottle. The postcard was sent by Edith who writes that the man in the doorway, in his shirtsleeves, is her father.

CRADLEY HEATH LEAGUE, 1921

The fine bunch of men on this postcard are proudly showing off their trophies. The wording on the board is made up of players' medals. The picture must have been taken after a very successful season - but at what sport? There is a hint that it was football, as one cup has a replica of a player on the lid, and it looks like a footballer with a ball at his feet. It is believed that the team is from the County Constabulary, but this fact has not been substantiated.

HIGH STREET, CRADLEY, c.1912

This view of High Street is looking down the hill at Cradley - not to be confused with Cradley Heath. The old bakery is halfway down this road. There was little activity when this photograph was taken by an unknown photographer - even all the shops seem to be shut.

HIGH STREET, COLLEY GATE, c.1912

Postcards of Colley Gate rarely turn up. Like the previous picture, this one is by an anonymous photographer. On the right is Woodall's shop, where they almost certainly traded in ladies' wear. A pile of rubble lies in the gutter in front of the shop, but there is no indication as to the reason for this - perhaps alterations were in progress on the premises. There are several people walking up the hill, away from the camera.

Making "Nuts" in the Black Country.

MAKING NUTS IN THE BLACK COUNTRY, c.1910

The manufacture of nuts and bolts was just one of the many local industries. This postcard, in the series published by John Price & Sons, depicts a typical forge and other antiquated machinery used in the making of nuts, bolts and nails. The factory workers used to work very long hours and received little reward at the end of the day.

One **MINE CHAIN,** $1\frac{1}{16}$ inch diameter ; length 3720 yards ; weight 23 tons, 13 cwt. 1 qr. 0 lbs.
The Carriers, (L. & N. W. Rly. Co.) state that this is the longest and heaviest chain in one length despatched from the Black Country for many years.

A MINE CHAIN, c.1920

Although the picture is not of a Black Country location, it is of interest because the chain was manufactured here. It was the longest and heaviest piece of chain - in one length - to come from a Black Country factory. It has been suggested that it was made at Eliza Tinsley's works, at Old Hill, but no proof of this has materialised. The postcard was published as an advertisement for the firm of Moffatt Brothers of High Street, Gateshead-on-Tyne.

BLACK-COUNTRY MINERS LEAVING THE PIT.

BLACK COUNTRY MINERS,
c.1912

This rare postcard shows miners leaving the pit - probably at the Earl of Dudley's colliery. The winding gear looks somewhat primitive and it seems that this particular pit was one of the shallower ones of the area. An overturned "bouk" lies in the background. Published by John Price & Sons of Bilston.

Dandy Pit Disaster. Pensnett Funeral Scenes.

DANDY PIT DISASTER, 29th April, 1923

One of the many tragic accidents in the area occurred at the Dandy Pit. near Pensnett, when five men lost their lives on the 21st April 1923. This postcard is one of a series that recorded the tragedy. It shows the funeral of three of the miners at Pensnett Church. Thousands of people turned out to line the route of the funeral procession, to pay their last respects to the victims of the disaster. The churchyard is shown packed with mourners.

Short Notice to Quit.

Owing to the Coal Mines in the Black Country, frequent subsidences of the surface take place, with very inconvenient results to property, as shown above.

"SHORT NOTICE TO QUIT", c.1908

This postcard gives further evidence of the subsidence that mining caused in the area. A loaded horse-drawn vehicle is moving a family's possessions as they are given "Short Notice to Quit". There is nothing to identify this particular area of the Black Country but, again, this is one of John Price's publications.